Great Big Animals

HUGE POLAR BEARS

By Stephanie Carrington

Gareth Stevens
PUBLISHING

Please visit our website, www.garethstevens.com. For a free color catalog of all our high-quality books, call toll free 1-800-542-2595 or fax 1-877-542-2596.

Cataloging-in-Publication Data

Names: Carrington, Stephanie.
Title: Huge polar bears / Stephanie Carrington.
Description: New York : Gareth Stevens Publishing, 2018. | Series: Great big animals | Includes index.
Identifiers: ISBN 9781538209035 (pbk.) | ISBN 9781538209059 (library bound) | ISBN 9781538209042 (6 pack)
Subjects: LCSH: Polar bear–Juvenile literature.
Classification: LCC QL737.C27 C37 2018 | DDC 599.786–dc23

First Edition

Published in 2018 by
Gareth Stevens Publishing
111 East 14th Street, Suite 349
New York, NY 10003

Copyright © 2018 Gareth Stevens Publishing

Editor: Kate Mikoley
Designer: Sarah Liddell

Photo credits: Cover, p. 1 seafarer/Shutterstock.com; pp. 5, 15 NaturesMomentsuk/Shutterstock.com; p. 7 Vladimir Melnik/Shutterstock.com; p. 9 Sergey Uryadnikov/Shutterstock.com; p. 11 FloridaStock/Shutterstock.com; pp. 13, 24 (fur) Zhiltsov Alexandr/Shutterstock.com; pp. 17, 24 (ice) Henri Vandelanotte/Shutterstock.com; p. 19 Fotokon/Shutterstock.com; p. 21 Johann Helgason/Shutterstock.com; pp. 23, 24 (cub) Gecko1968/Shutterstock.com.

All rights reserved. No part of this book may be reproduced in any form without permission in writing from the publisher, except by a reviewer.

Printed in China

CPSIA compliance information: Batch #CW18GS: For further information contact Gareth Stevens, New York, New York at 1-800-542-2595.

Contents

Big Bears. 4

It's Freezing! 14

Super Swimmers 18

Words to Know 24

Index. 24

Polar bears are so big!

5

Some are 8 feet long.

7

They're the biggest bear.

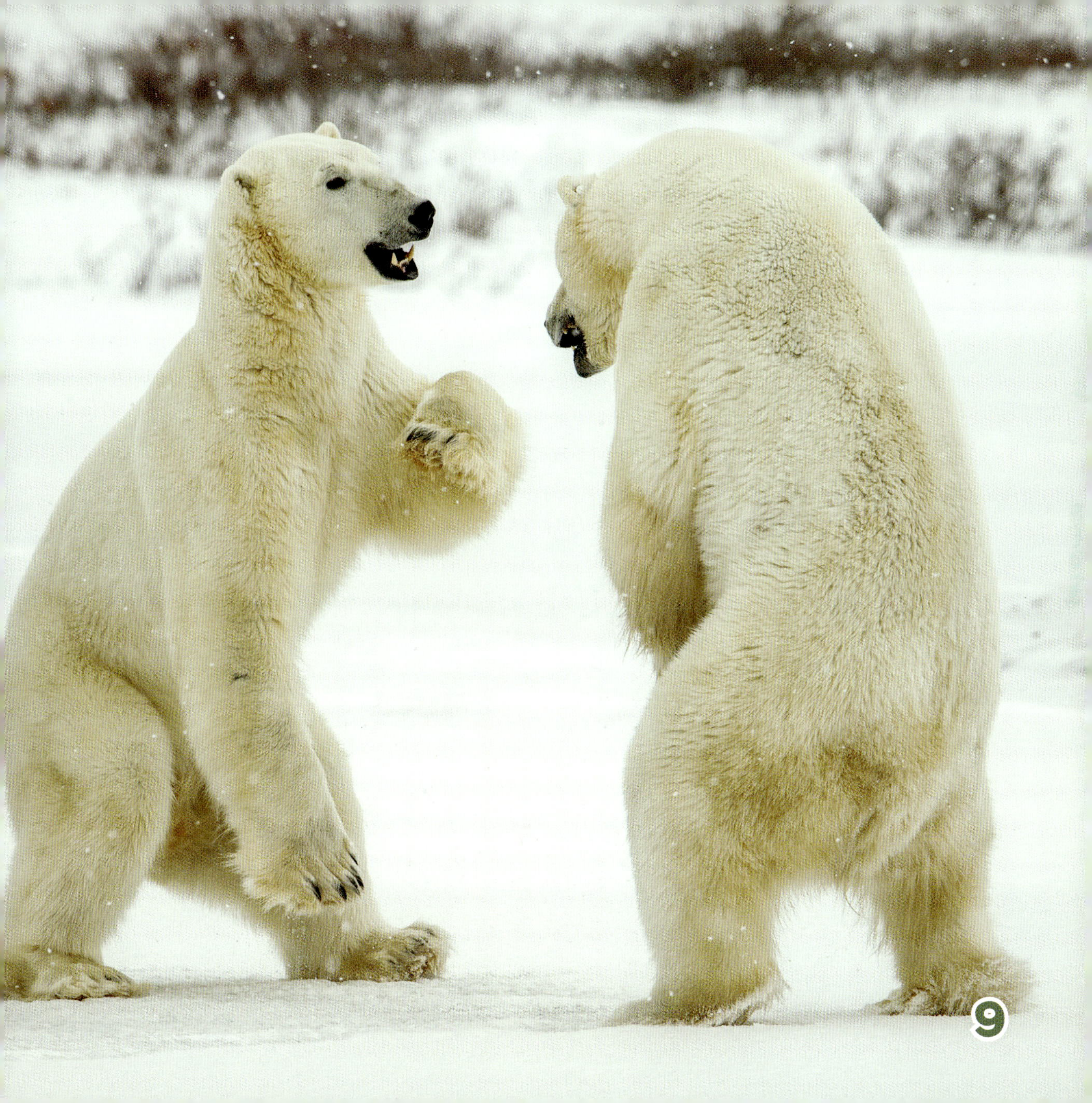

Some weigh more than 1,500 pounds.

11

Polar bears have fur.
It looks white.

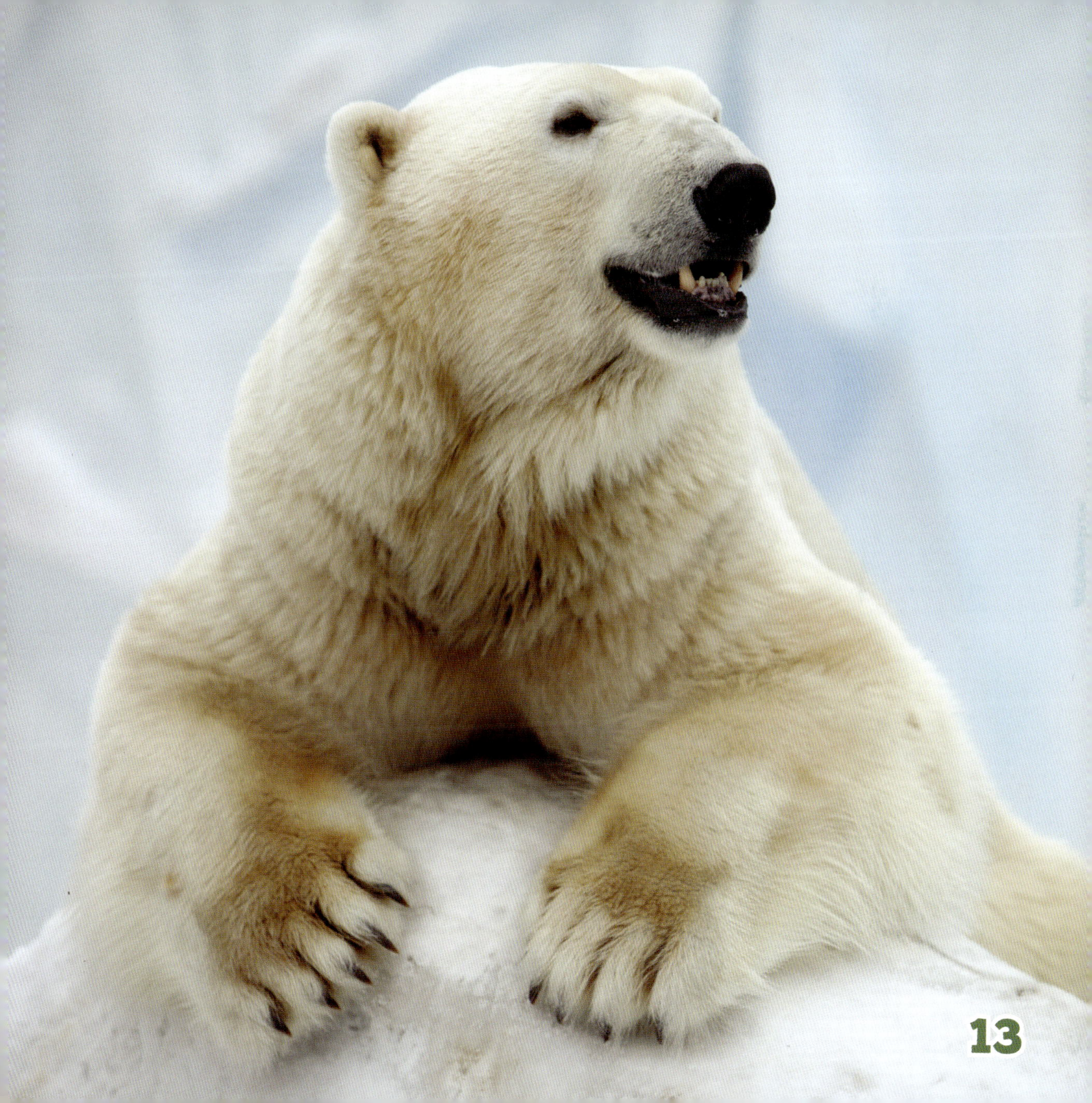

Polar bears like the cold.

15

They live by the sea.
Many live on sea ice.

17

Polar bears love to swim.

19

They eat other animals.

21

Baby polar bears are called cubs.

23

Words to Know

cub  fur  ice

Index

cubs 22 ice 16

fur 12 sea 16